THE BODY A[T THE]

Heart

written by
D.M. Brock & **Monica Ashour**

designed by
David Fiegenschue & **Emily Gudde**

Level 7
BOOK 2
Second Edition

TOBET THEOLOGY OF THE BODY EVANGELIZATION TEAM

Dedicated to the Church, including our family and friends, and especially to Mother Mary and Saint John Paul. Tremendous thanks to all TOBET members over the years. Special thanks to Joseph, Kathy, Michael, Patrick, and Sheryl. We are grateful for consultation work by the translator of the *Theology of the Body*, Dr. Michael Waldstein, as well as Dr. Susan Waldstein. We are also grateful for the consultation work of Katrina J. Zeno, MTS.

For Garland and Helen Brock

Nihil Obstat: Tomas Fuerte, S.T.L.
Censor Librorum

Imprimatur: +Most Reverend Samuel J. Aquila, S.T.L.
Archbishop of Denver
Denver, Colorado, USA
Feast of Sts. Joachim and Ann
July 26, 2019

Library of Congress information on file. ISBN 978-1-945845-37-6 • Second Edition
Cover Design: FigDesign • Layout: Emily Gudde • Editor: Dayspring Brock • Associate Editor: Alexis Mausolf

Excerpts from the English translation of the *Catechism of the Catholic Church*. New York: Catholic Book Publishing Co., 1994.
The quote on p. 28 is from John Paul II. *Dominum et Vivificantem—On the Holy Spirit in the Life of the Church and the World*. Rome: The Holy See, May 18, 1986. w2.vatican.va/content/john-paul-ii/en/encyclicals/documents/hf_jp-ii_enc_18051986_dominum-et-vivificantem.html.
Based on John Paul II's *Man and Woman He Created Them: A Theology of the Body*. Trans. Michael Waldstein, Copyright © 2006. Used by permission of Pauline Books & Media, 50 Saint Paul's Ave, Boston, Massachusetts 02130. All rights reserved. www.pauline.org.
Kowalska, St. Maria Faustina. *Divine Mercy In My Soul—Diary of Sister M. Faustina Kowalska*, entry 72. Stockbridge, Massachusetts: Marian Press, 2003.
All Scripture verses are from the *New American Bible*, Revised Edition (NABRE).
Excerpts from *YOUCAT*. Trans. Michael J. Miller. (San Francisco: Ignatius Press, 2011), www.ignatius.com. Used with permission.
Image Credits: Shutterstock: pg 4 ©Everett Historical / pg 9 ©SThom / pg 10 ©Kirill Kurashov / pg 11 ©Siberia Video and Photo / pg 12 ©Monkey Business Images / pg 13 ©shaineast / pg 14 ©moosehenderson / pg 16 ©Andrey Burmakin / pg 18 ©G-Stock Studio / pg 19 ©Zwiebackesser / pg 20 ©feliks / pg 21 (camo pattern) ©CoSveta / pg 22 ©Lidia Muhamadeeva / pg 25 ©3Dimka / pg 26 ©Dennis Sabo / pg 28 ©Pressmaster / pg 30-31 ©FrankHH / pg 33 (tree vector) ©alazur / pg 34 ©FXQuadro / pg 36 ©PENPAK PROMLEE / pg 37 ©Filip Fuxa / pg 40 ©wavebreakmedia / pg 42 ©michaeljung / pg 44 ©BokehStore / pg 45 ©zimmytws / pg 47 ©Renata Sedmakova / pg 48 ©Andy Dean Photography

Printed in the United States of America. © Copyright 2021 Monica Ashour. All rights reserved. No part of this book may be reproduced or transmitted in any form or by any means, electronic or mechanical, including photocopying, recording, or by any information storage and retrieval system without permission in writing from the publisher.

TOBET PRESS

Table of Contents

1 **The Heart as a Battlefield** — 4
- The heart is the seat of the person.
- After The Fall, the heart became vulnerable to sin.
- Evaluating the inner movements of the heart helps to conquer sin.

2 **The Battleplan of the Heart** — 12
- Devising a strategy to resist temptation helps conquer concupiscence.
- Natural Law leads to understanding God's design.
- Revelation forms the heart to love.

3 **Pledging Your Heart** — 24
- By maturing in a relationship with Christ, one will develop an "ethos of the heart."
- A person's understanding of God is linked to his or her understanding of identity.
- A secure identity in God yields freedom.

4 **Entering the Battle** — 36
- A violation of conscience comes from detachment.
- Self-mastery and reverence lead to true love.
- Devotion to Jesus and Mary strengthens purity.

1 The Heart as a Battlefield

The Heart at War

You have probably read about war in books, or have seen photographs or documentaries. War often arises between nations, rulers, or tribes when they cannot agree about land, borders, treasure, or beliefs. But these are not the only wars we fight.

Did you know that your heart is also at war? As soon as you were baptized, there began a war for your heart. You may not be aware of it, but your heart is a battlefield. Are you prepared for the fight of your life?

The Heart Is You

What is the heart? Biologically speaking, the heart is an organ that pumps your blood. But symbolically speaking, the heart is the deepest part of you. For centuries, people have described the heart as the depth of the self—where you experience the strongest forces like loss, hope, or belief. The heart is that place where you are most afraid or most confident.

The heart is also where you make choices, especially the choice to love. Some have described it as the place where the "real you" is seated. The Church says the heart is the "inner sanctuary" where the voice of God speaks. This is where your inner battles are fought, for your very identity in Christ resides in the heart.

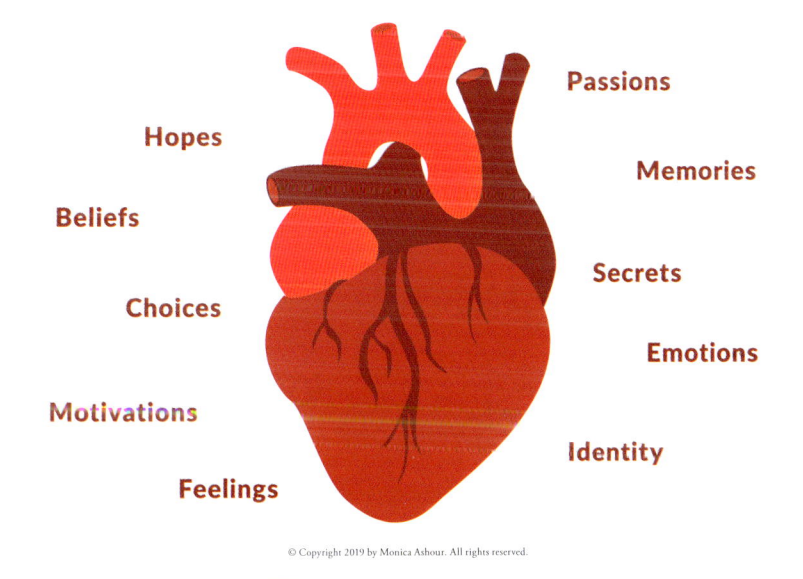

Hopes
Beliefs
Choices
Motivations
Feelings

Passions
Memories
Secrets
Emotions
Identity

© Copyright 2019 by Monica Ashour. All rights reserved.

"The 'heart' has become a battlefield between love and concupiscence."   TOB 32:3

> "Constituted in a state of holiness, man was destined to be fully 'divinized' by God in glory. Seduced by the devil, he wanted to be like God, but without God...."
> *CCC 398*

The True You

Ultimately, your deepest identity is as son or daughter of God, loved and cherished by your good and protective Father in Heaven. If we fully understood and accepted this, love would always win in our hearts. There would be no battlefield; we could live in perfect peace and holiness. So what stops us from embracing this truth?

Heart Attack

We often fail to accept our identity because we face an Enemy. His aim is to separate you from the Father and to rob you of your inheritance as God's child. This Enemy is a deceiver, a serpent, a fallen angel. Just as he led Adam and Eve away from God and their true purpose and design, he tries to lead you away too. Know your enemy; know that your heart is under attack. You might call it a spiritual "heart attack."

The Heart:

Where Sin Begins

BUT

Where Love Can Win!

© Copyright 2019 by Monica Ashour. All rights reserved.

> "...[T]hanks be to God that, although you were once slaves of sin, you have become obedient from the heart...."
>
> Rom 6:17

Change of Heart

The human heart has long been under attack, but in the beginning of time, this was not so. Before Adam and Eve sinned, their hearts were holy. They saw each other and all of creation as gifts to be cherished, and they saw God as a good Gift-Giver Whom they could trust.

Adam and Eve had complete freedom to love. They could eat and sing and laugh and even play with the animals for as long as they wished. They had no desire to choose anything other than what was good. In their heart of hearts they knew their deepest identity was as children of God. They had complete union with Him, with each other, with nature, and within themselves—body and spirit.

The Heart's Fall

Before The Fall	After The Fall
Union	Disunion
Freedom	Enslavement
Desire for good	Desire for sin
Loving others	Using others

© Copyright 2019 by Monica Ashour. All rights reserved.

Then the Enemy whispered lies to Adam and Eve, planting seeds of doubt about God. Sin took root in their hearts, affecting their choices and bodily actions. They no longer acted with complete freedom. They no longer had perfect union, but disunion. They now had the tendency and desire to sin. They forgot their identity.

> "For all that is in the world, sensual lust, enticement for the eyes, and a pretentious life, is not from the Father but is from the world."
>
> 1 Jn. 2:16

Broken Heart

How did sin change humanity? We have all inherited Original Sin from Adam and Eve. Rather than wholeness, we experience brokenness; rather than freedom, we experience enslavement; rather than bliss, we experience pain. Our hardest battles are against our sinful selves. We struggle with impurity, which leads us to see persons as objects for our own gratification. Ultimately, we make ourselves "gods."

That tendency toward selfishness is called concupiscence (kon-KEW-pe-sense), an inclination or "leaning into" sin. Although Baptism washes away Original Sin, we still experience sin's effects through concupiscence and the fallen world.

St. John Paul identified three types of concupiscence: that of the eyes, the flesh, and the pride of life.

The Three-Fold Concupiscence

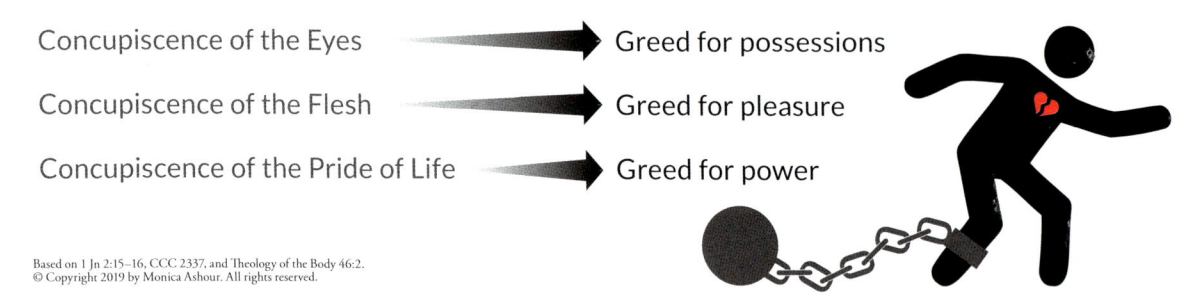

Concupiscence of the Eyes ⟶ Greed for possessions

Concupiscence of the Flesh ⟶ Greed for pleasure

Concupiscence of the Pride of Life ⟶ Greed for power

Based on 1 Jn 2:15–16, CCC 2337, and Theology of the Body 46:2.
© Copyright 2019 by Monica Ashour. All rights reserved.

Heart Taken Hostage

Why do we sin? Is it because we desire failure or want to feel pain? No. We sin for temporary gratification. We are duped into sin by its promise of possessions, pleasure, or power.

One way sin works on the heart is when good things begin to control us. Have you ever become so obsessed with playing a video game, or so set on wearing a certain brand of clothing, that you could think of nothing else? Are your thoughts consumed with those people that you find attractive? Do you work obsessively to gain their attention? Or, do you dream of becoming the most popular in class, having the highest grades, or receiving the most athletic awards? Why? Though born of healthy desire, these dreams can become distorted and obsessive. They become rooted in selfishness.

Sports, attraction, and excelling in school are all good things. But when these things begin to occupy our hearts, leaving room for nothing else, they turn into temptations for greed, lust, and prestige.

Because of concupiscence, God's creation, which should be our ally, becomes a weapon in the hands of the Enemy. Created things that become idols imprison our hearts.

When we allow desires to master our hearts instead of our hearts mastering our desires, then we have a hostage situation.

Examining the Heart

So, how do we avoid being taken hostage? How can we defend our hearts from the Enemy? St. John Paul gives us some guidance. The first thing we must do to conquer concupiscence is to become aware of the inner movements of our hearts. In other words, instead of acting upon fleeting feelings, we should pause to identify our motives and evaluate what is happening inside.

Do any of these sound familiar?
- When you boast about that 100% on your history test, are you thinking about the feelings of your classmates, or only about yourself?
- When you devise a scheme to exclude someone from your kickball team, are you acting out of love or jealousy?
- When you find yourself cutting in line every chance you get, are you considering others, or only yourself?

When you become aware of the inner movements of your heart, you can choose to do good. Freedom then is yours.

"Thus, Christ appeals to the inner man."
Theology of the Body 24:4

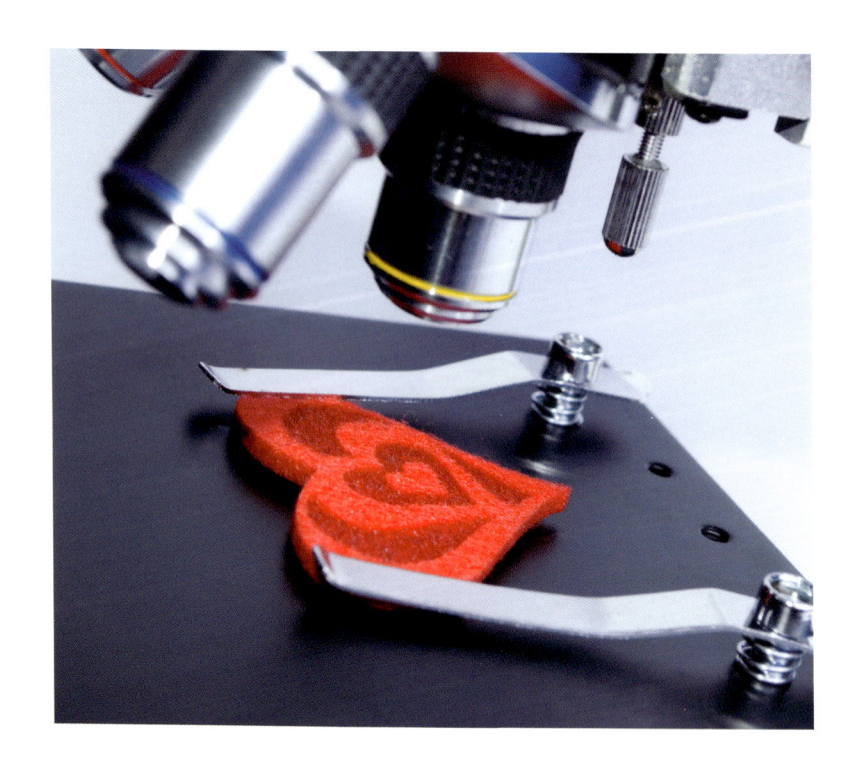

The Choice

Have you ever felt like a character in a TV show with a devil and an angel perched on your shoulders, urging you toward sin or toward virtue? Your heart often experiences a tug of war between right and wrong. You can win the battle against sin by pausing to identify the inner movements of your heart, and then by making the choice to love.

Points to Ponder:
1. Which kind of concupiscence do you see as the most troubling in the culture around you—concupiscence of the eyes, the flesh, or the pride of life?
2. When was the last time you were tempted to do something wrong, but you chose to do good instead? Were you aware of the freedom you felt when you chose to act virtuously?

Mission: Take one hour of your day today and focus on the inner movements of your heart. If you are with your classmates, notice if you experience the temptation to make fun of someone. Then evaluate this choice. How can you choose virtue? If a classmate tempts you to disrupt a teacher, what is the right thing to do? At home, will you find ways to stay on your computer all evening, or will you decide to play with your little siblings instead? Being aware of the inner movements of your heart takes practice, but the more you do so, the stronger you will grow against sin and the easier it will be to choose virtue.

2 The Battleplan of the Heart

The Un-formed Heart

There is a war being fought for your heart. Can you stand against the forces of concupiscence? Do you have a battleplan?

Sports players act like...

My youth leader says...

Video games show me...

Movies teach me...

The music I listen to makes me feel...

My parents tell me...

Battling Temptation

Look at the boy on the previous page and the various forces fighting for his heart. Which will win? He will most likely listen to the voice that is the loudest. This may or may not be a voice of virtue.

For example, if he really respects his parents, he will consider their advice first. But if he allows the concupiscence of the flesh to speak loudest, he will probably choose to click on impure images on his computer.

Do you see how important it is to have a plan when temptation strikes? You need a strategy to win against the Enemy. You need a battleplan for your heart.

"A clean heart create for me, God; renew within me a steadfast spirit." — Ps. 51:12

Sources of Truth

There are two sources that can be trusted to form our hearts: Natural Law and Revelation. Natural Law is based on God's design of creation. Revelation is God's plan of salvation for us, as revealed by Sacred Scripture and Sacred Tradition, and guided by the Magisterium of the Church. Both are very important for a Theology of the Body worldview. Let's begin with Natural Law.

The Battleplan and Natural Law

By simply observing nature, we can study the design of the Creator. For example, it is natural for a bird to fly and for a fish to swim. If an eagle tried to swim in a river or a trout attempted to fly over a mountain, both would die. Why? Because it is not in their natures to do so. An eagle is not designed to swim, nor a trout to fly. When eagles and trout act in accord with their designs, they flourish.

Wouldn't it be strange if we tried to train the eagle and the trout to defy their natures and learn each other's skills? Is the eagle less free because it cannot swim? And is the trout's life worthless because it has to live in the ocean rather than the air? By no means! We respect that the eagle has not been designed for the water, nor the trout for the atmosphere.

Humans have also been given a specific design. This design has great benefits but also some limits. We cannot fly, nor can we live underwater. However, we are capable of much more. We are higher than all of creation, for our nature is to love.

Natural Law of the Body

Bodily Action	Response of the Body
drinking poison	difficulty breathing, confusion, death
not eating	starvation, organs stop functioning, death
looking at impure images	addiction, objectifying others, inability to have real intimacy
cheating on schoolwork	anxiety, lack of learning and mental focus, apathy

© Copyright 2019 by Monica Ashour. All rights reserved.

Consider what happens when we fight against or ignore the design of the body. Notice how the body responds to each of the actions in the chart above. There are limits to our design. We can trust the body to be a guide because nature is a guide. The Creator stands behind His creation.

When we submit to God's design for the body, we wield a great weapon against the Enemy, who is a liar and the Father of Lies. The Enemy likes to lie to us especially about the human body. He wants to persuade us to disregard our nature. Yet, when we respect the design of the body, our hearts are freed by truth.

The Truth about Lying

The natural design of the body can direct us to what is morally right or wrong. For example, Natural Law shows us that lying is wrong based on the body's reaction. Lie detectors can measure physical responses such as increased heart rate, respiration, eye movement, and voice modulation that occur when a person tells a lie. Lying goes against the body.

Personal experience can also teach us about the physical and mental consequences of lying—the regret, the fear of being found out, the anxiety. Even if someone was never taught "thou shalt not lie," he or she could still come to the same conclusion: lying distresses the body and harms relationships.

The Rehab of the Heart

When we oppose the Natural Law, we harm ourselves and the world. But there is hope— our hearts can go to rehab! God is the merciful Physician, Who wants to forgive and heal us. Read the example on the next page to see how the heart can be healed through rehabilitation.

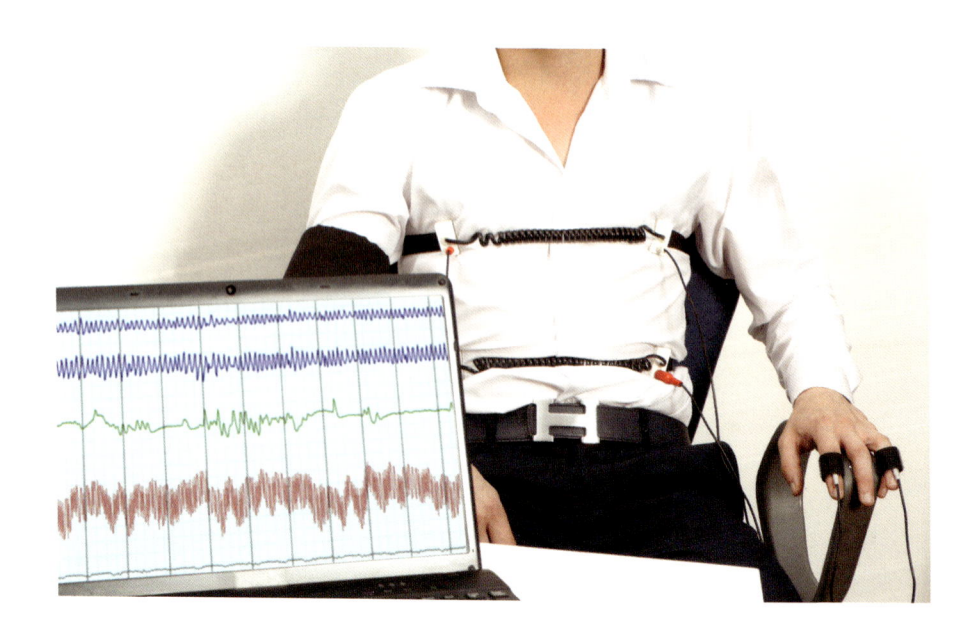

Reading the spiral from outside to inside:

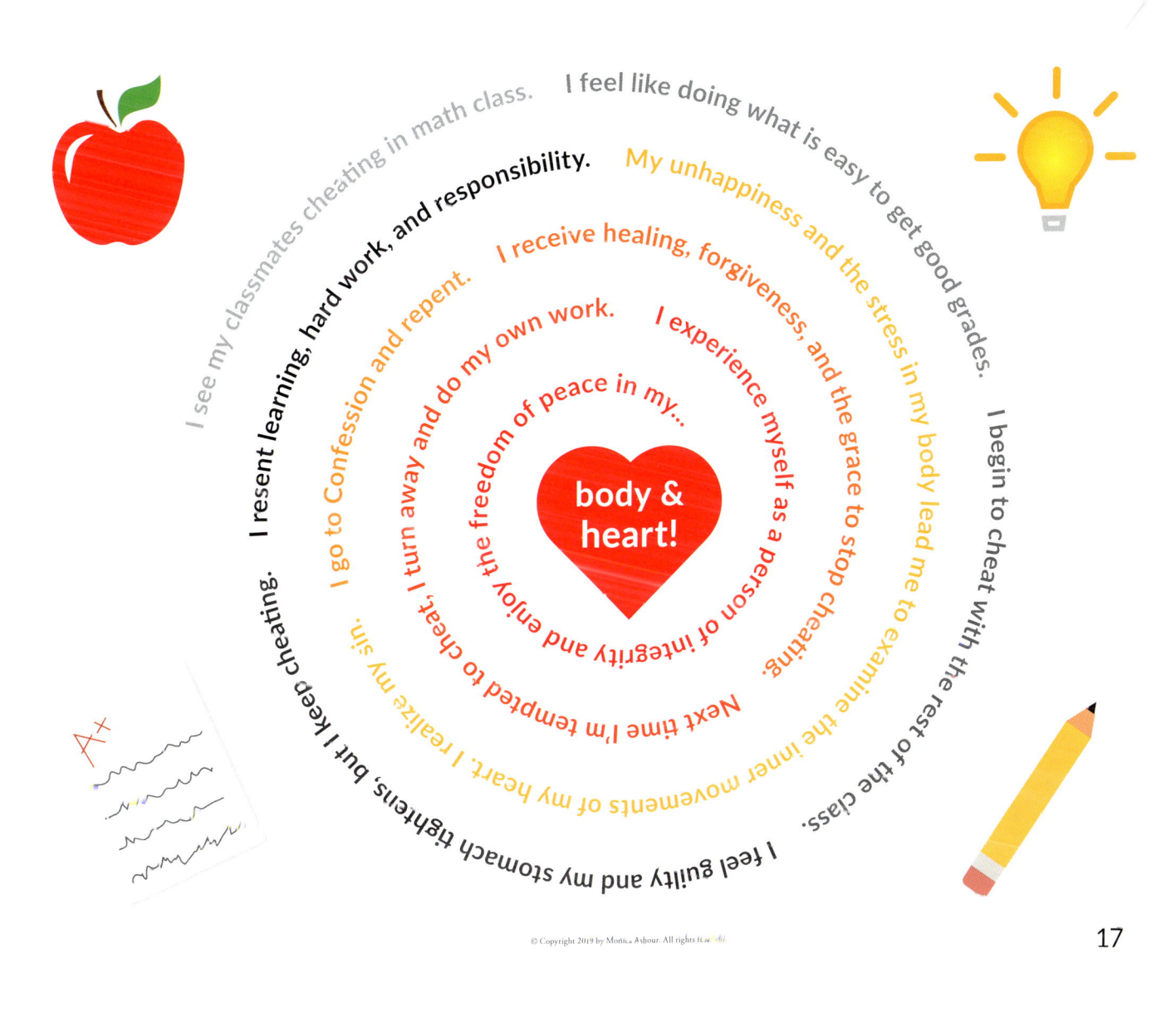

- I see my classmates cheating in math class.
- I feel like doing what is easy to get good grades.
- I begin to cheat with the rest of the class.
- I feel guilty and my stomach tightens, but I keep cheating.
- I resent learning, hard work, and responsibility.
- My unhappiness and the stress in my body lead me to examine the inner movements of my heart. I realize my sin.
- I go to Confession and repent.
- Next time I'm tempted to cheat, I turn away and do my own work.
- I receive healing, forgiveness, and the grace to stop cheating.
- I experience myself as a person of integrity and enjoy the freedom of peace in my... body & heart!

17

Made for Others

One of the Enemy's greatest lies is that we are made to please only ourselves. This is simply not true. Instead, the body reveals the greatest purpose of our design: that is, we are made **for** others.

What do our bodies tell us? Our hands are made for helping, our arms for holding, and our faces are made to communicate with others. We can know this by simply observing the design of the body.

People are meant to live together in community. In fact, humans find their greatest meaning in the **gift of self**—loving others by sacrificing something of themselves, whether it be time spent, possessions shared, or hearts exchanged. Natural Law leads toward human love within God's plan.

"[T]he human heart [can] accept even difficult demands in the name of love, for an ideal, and above all *in the name of love for a person*...."   *Theology of the Body 79:9*

The Battleplan and Revelation

Natural Law is one phase of the battleplan, but humanity needs something more. When left to ourselves, we often choose to contradict the truth of the body and let sin overcome us. So God has given us Revelation, the second part of the battleplan.

The highest point of Revelation is God's love made visible through Jesus' Gift of Self on the cross. In an extraordinary act, God sent His Son, Jesus Christ, to disarm Satan and defeat him with his own weapon! What is the Enemy's greatest weapon? Death. The Son of God laid down His life freely, and by rising from the dead, He conquered death. Death was defeated by Life and Love.

"For God so loved the world that he gave his only Son, so that everyone who believes in him might not perish but might have eternal life." Jn. 3:16

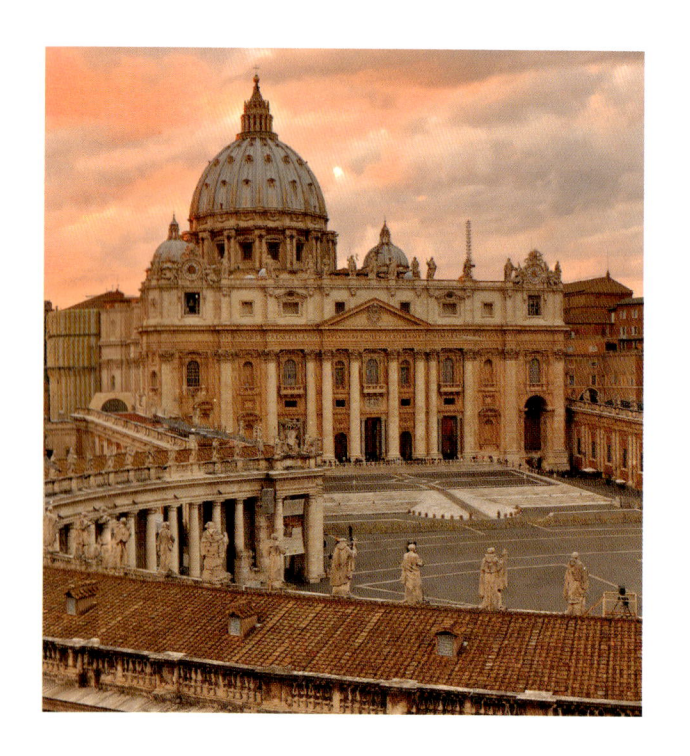

The Church Upholds Revelation

The Church, founded by the risen Lord, continues Christ's mission of bringing love to the world.

Have you ever seen the colonnades at St. Peter's Basilica in Rome? They are meant to symbolize the arms of Mother Church welcoming us and guiding us to the Truth. Just like a good mother, the Church leads her children to Christ. Mother Church "hands down" Scripture and Tradition, which is what the word *tradition* literally means.

With over 2,000 years of strategies for forming the heart, the Church has all you need to take down the Enemy who is trying to steal your heart. The Church helps you understand the battleplan and provides you with abundant weapons and supplies to win the war for your heart.

"He is before all things, and in him all things hold together. He is the head of the body, the church...."
Col. 1:17–18

Battleplan = Natural Law & Revelation
Soldiers = Christians
Supplies = Sacraments
Drills = Prayers

Map = Scripture
Armor = Tradition
Officers = Magisterium
Secret Weapon = Holy Spirit

Surrendering to God, Not the Enemy

What would happen if a soldier decided the battleplan did not apply to him? What if he made up his own rules? That would be mutiny! Sometimes we approach God's commands in a similarly foolish way. We might feel that God's rules only make life more burdensome. Going to Confession or loving our neighbor can feel difficult.

But as we begin to surrender to these good habits, we grow in maturity. We start to see that God's rules are good for us. We can trust the rules because God knows us better than we know ourselves. He knows the Enemy better too. God's rules found in Scripture and Tradition are for our good.

Lift up your Hearts

Whenever you go to Mass, have a "heart-to-Heart" conversation with God. Some of the most powerful words of the Liturgy are when we say that we lift our hearts "up to the Lord." The next time you say this at Mass, really focus on lifting your heart up to God. What concerns, fears, feelings, or hopes might you offer to Christ? The Mass is the highest point of our lives, for there we enter into Calvary where Jesus Christ fought for us on the cross. Jesus wants to receive your embattled heart and set it free.

He has won the war! All we have to do is accept His victory. We gain a share in His victory by receiving the Eucharist, the Body of Christ. This gives us "Bread for the journey" which will fortify us against the Enemy in our battle.

When your heart is properly formed with the battleplan of Natural Law and Revelation, you will know the truth, and the truth will set you free (see John 8:32).

Points to Ponder:
1. Think about the voices that tempt you the most when you are in the midst of a battle. What's your strategy?
2. Can you elaborate on the military metaphor (pg. 21) for Catholicism? Are there parallels for other aspects of our Faith, like relics, martyrs, sacramentals, feast days, or Mother Mary?

Mission: What messages do you hear everyday that contradict the truth of the body? Do you know where to go for answers? What does God's Word say? What does the Church say? Are you able to back up the truth of the body with both Natural Law and Revelation?

3 Pledging Your Heart

Connecting the Dots

Have you ever stared at a 3-D picture until you were able to see the image underneath? Your eyes glaze over the patterns and dots until, finally, it all makes sense, and a picture appears! You may have a similar sensation as you journey deeper into the Catholic Faith.

Sometimes it might seem that God's laws are a random series of dots, unrelated to reality. But as you mature in your relationship with Christ and come to own the truth in your heart, you will begin to see a beautiful picture emerge. It is God's law of love.

> "The entire law of the Gospel is contained in the 'New Commandment' of Jesus to love one another as he has loved us." *CCC 1970*

25

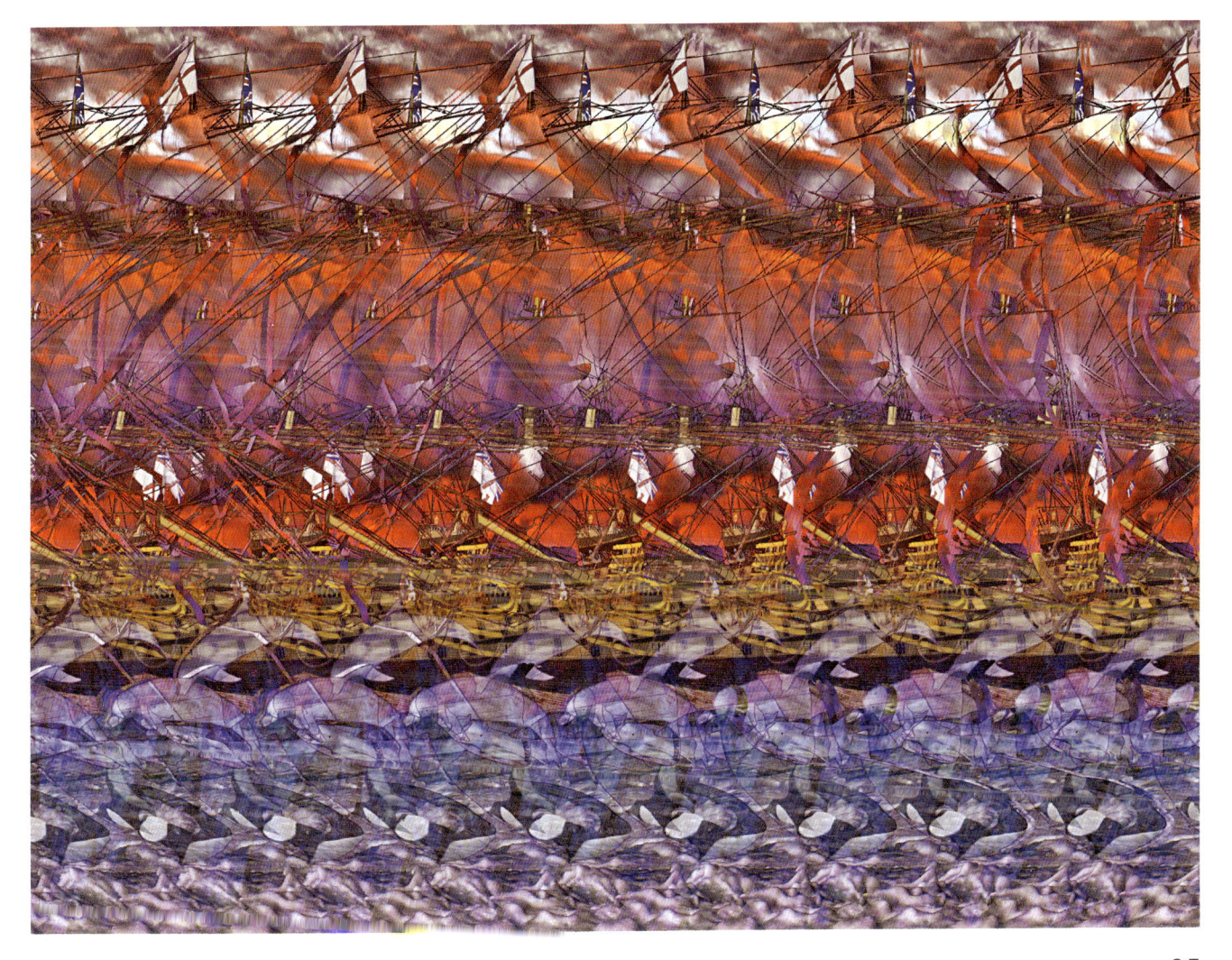

Knowing but Not Owning

Maddie went to her youth group every Sunday night and could answer all the catechism questions. But on Monday, when the girls on her soccer team made fun of one of her friends, she laughed along with them, even though she knew it was wrong.

Nicholas read the lives of saints with his family and sometimes thought of himself as a soldier of Christ, like St. Ignatius of Loyola. But when he heard some boys in the band mocking the Catholic Church, he hoped no one would remember that he was Catholic.

Why were Maddie and Nicholas tongue-tied? They knew the truth, so why didn't they defend it when put to the test? Were they just cowardly? Perhaps the problem was deeper.

Even though their hearts had been formed in the Faith, Maddie and Nicholas had not yet **owned** the truth. They had not yet pledged their hearts to Christ the King. So, when their beliefs were challenged, they retreated from the battle.

The Longest Journey

Some people get stuck in the stage of forming the heart and never take the next step to **own** what they believe. Consider the following: Is an army more effective when it drafts citizens and forces them to fight as soldiers, or when it is made up of those who freely volunteer to defend their country with their lives? On the battlefield of your heart, which kind of Christian soldier do you want to be? One who fights half-heartedly, or one who is whole-heartedly engaged in the battle?

Sometimes the longest journey is from the head to the heart. Even when we know the teachings of the Faith, we might not be convinced of their truth. To be wholehearted for Christ means knowing Him personally and having a friendship with Him. Then, suddenly, the tenets of the Church seem to come alive because they lead you to a deeper encounter with Christ. You will want to follow them because you want to follow Him! The Truth is not a list of "do's and don'ts"; the Truth is a Person—the Word made flesh, Jesus Christ.

From Head to Heart

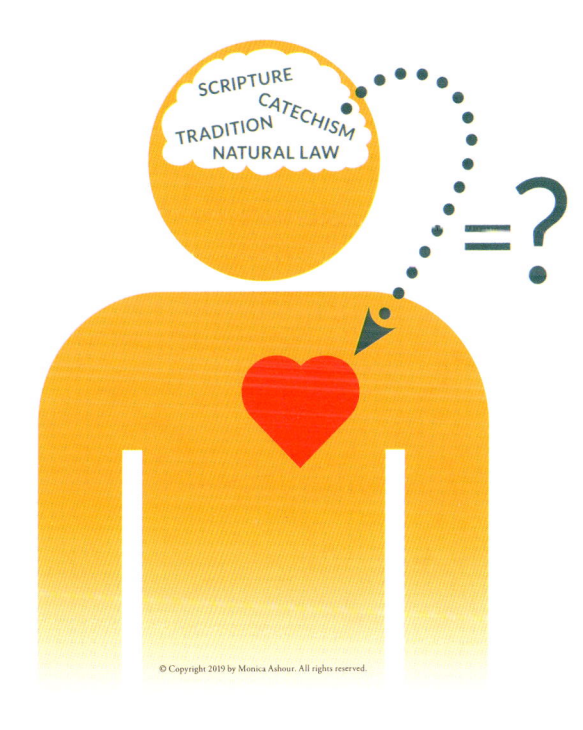

"...[V]irtuous character...is determined not so much by faithfulness to an impersonal 'natural law,' but to the personal Creator...."
Theology of the Body 124:6

"And faith, in its deepest essence, is the openness of the human heart to the gift: to God's self-communication in the Holy Spirit." *Dominum et Vivificantem, 51*

The Ethos of the Heart

St. John Paul coined the phrase "ethos of the heart," which means making God's truth your own. When you allow God's laws to penetrate your heart, they are no longer abstract rules that you must obey. Instead, they become personal and alive to you; obeying God's laws becomes your expression of love for Christ.

So how do you develop an ethos of the heart? Ask the Holy Spirit to help you own God's law of love in your heart. The Holy Spirit is like a defibrillator for the human spirit. He shocks your heart into love!

When you allow Him to work in you, He will grant you an ethos of the heart. In other words, you will be able to pledge your loyalty to the battleplan. For most people, this does not happen overnight; it can be a long process. However, the more you learn to trust the Holy Spirit, the more you will own the truth.

Trusting God

Having an ethos of the heart requires being confident in your identity. Identity is based in belonging. You belong to your family and friends. But most of all, you belong to God. So the key to knowing yourself is knowing Who God is.

What is your experience of God the Father? Do you believe in your heart that He is trustworthy? Do you believe He is a good Gift-Giver Who loves you, His child, and provides for your needs? Girls, God wants you to claim your identity as His daughter. Boys, God wants you to claim your identity as His son. God's fatherly love is worthy of trust.

God the Father

Identity of Trust

Me

© Copyright 2019 by Monica Ashour. All rights reserved.

"'God, the Father of our Lord Jesus Christ' embraces men and women in his Son.... It is a mystery of fatherly love...."
Theology of the Body 95:5

Who Do You Say that I Am?

The following are four common misconceptions about God that may affect your identity. Ask yourself if you have ever misunderstood God in any of these ways.

Fairy-Godfather

Some people think of God as a Fairy-Godfather. They believe his job is to give them whatever they want and never withhold anything from them. They view prayer as a vending machine. They pray, and then expect God to answer their request immediately. When he does not do what they want, they become bitter, feeling helpless and confused.

Tyrant God

Others think of God as a tyrant who waits to catch people in sin and then condemns them to eternal punishment. Theirs is a God of justice without mercy. People who believe in a Tyrant God spend their whole lives running away in fear and shame, hoping God will not catch up with them.

Neither of these images of God is true. The true God is good. He knows our needs and extends to us His mercy.

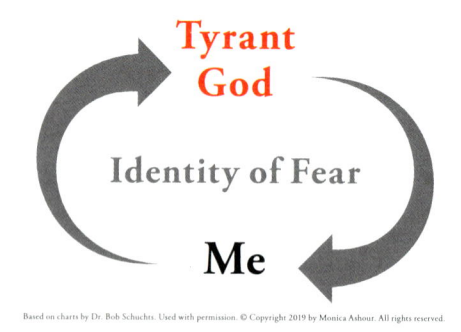

Fairy-Godfather God → Identity of Helplessness → Me

Tyrant God → Identity of Fear → Me

Based on charts by Dr. Bob Schuchts. Used with permission. © Copyright 2019 by Monica Ashour. All rights reserved.

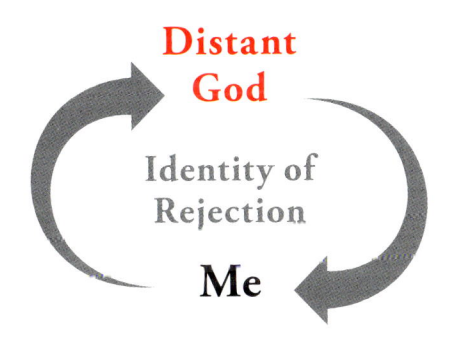

Distant God

Distant God / Identity of Rejection / **Me**

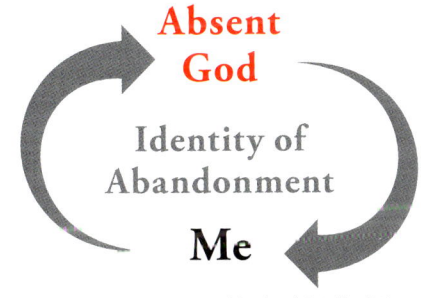

Absent God / Identity of Abandonment / **Me**

Based on charts by Dr. Bob Schuchts. Used with permission. © Copyright 2019 by Monica Ashour. All rights reserved.

Distant God
Some people experience God as a distant father who comes home periodically, pats them on the head, and leaves for more "important" work. This view of God can prevent people from seeking him. They are not convinced that God loves them enough to stick around, so they feel rejected and not worthy of love.

Absent God
Some people feel that God is absent. They don't understand why others are so full of faith while they themselves feel abandoned. In their loneliness, they wonder where God is.

However, God is neither distant nor absent. God is always present. He is Emmanuel—"God with us."

He is a loving Father Who has counted every hair on your head, Who has knit you in your mother's womb, and Who has engraved you in the palm of His hand. As Scripture says, "'For I know the plans I have for you,' declares the Lord, 'plans to prosper you and not to harm you, plans to give you hope and a future'" (Jer. 29:11).

31

> "For 'In him we live and move and have our being....'" — Acts 17:28

False Identity

If you have a false view of God, you may have a false view of yourself. For example, if you believe God to be a tyrant, you might think you are not a lovable person. False identities can also come from others. If someone says something cruel to you, do not allow those words to take root in your heart. Reject the falsehood, and embrace your identity as a child of God.

True Identity

Just as a medic treats injured soldiers on the battlefield, Jesus can heal our identity wounds. He Himself was mocked and called names, and though hurt, He never lost sight of His true identity as Son of the Father. And since He lives in you and you in Him, you can be secure in your true identity, no matter what happens in life.

His Heart to Your Heart

GRACE

UNDERSTOOD
EMPOWERED
CONNECTED
ACCEPTED
SECURE
PURE

© Copyright 2019 by Monica Ashour. All rights reserved.

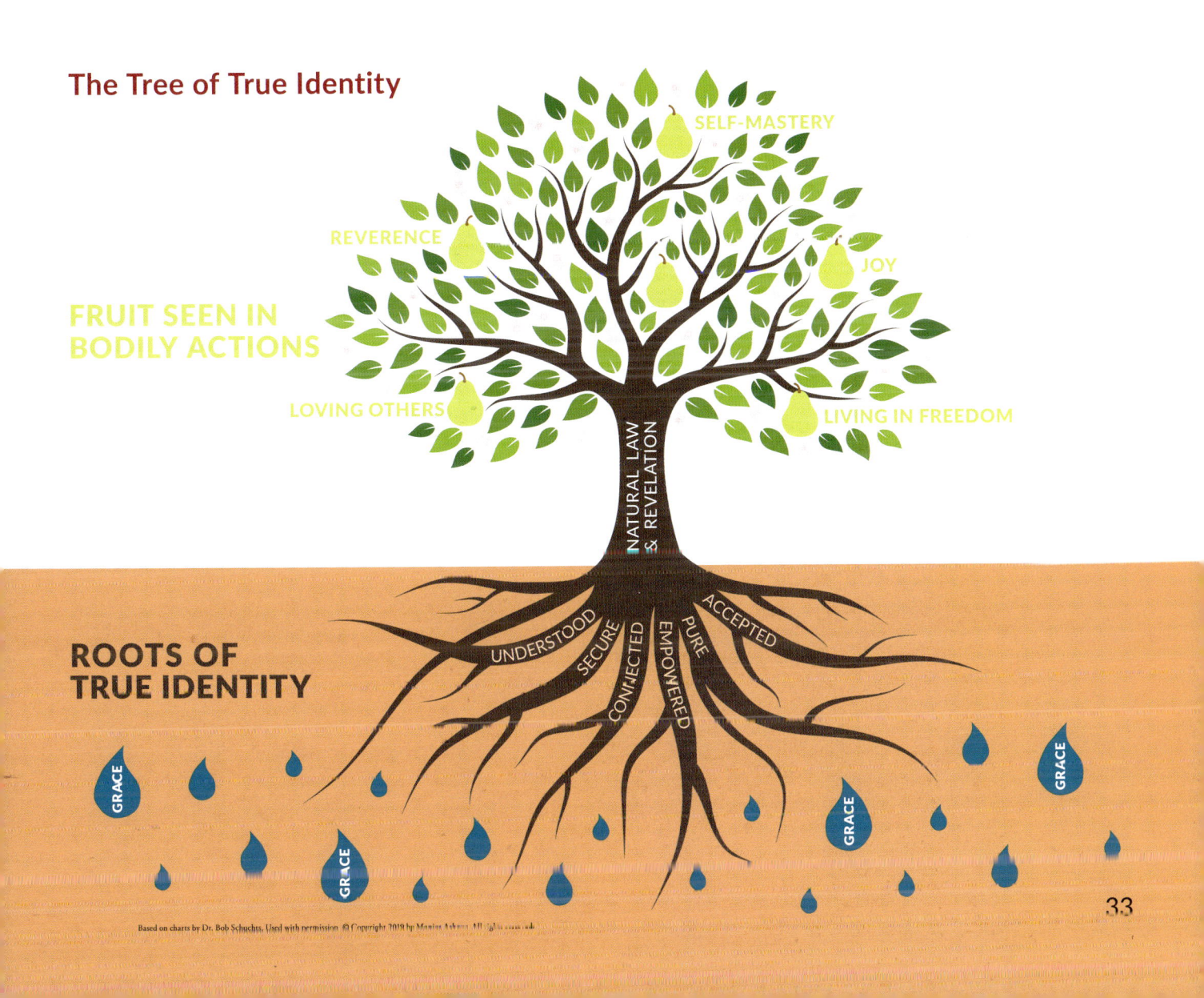

The Tree of True Identity

FRUIT SEEN IN BODILY ACTIONS

- SELF-MASTERY
- REVERENCE
- JOY
- LOVING OTHERS
- LIVING IN FREEDOM

NATURAL LAW & REVELATION

ROOTS OF TRUE IDENTITY

- UNDERSTOOD
- SECURE
- CONNECTED
- EMPOWERED
- PURE
- ACCEPTED

GRACE

33

Your Band of Brothers and Sisters

Don't forget that the Mystical Body of Christ can help you own your true identity. You are not alone! All those alive in Christ—in Heaven, on Earth, and in Purgatory—are fighting alongside of you.

Even the toughest soldier on a mission has the rest of his platoon behind him. Behind you is an army of saints in Heaven who have fought and won. When you are weary, you can ask for their intercession. They will pray for you to have the strength to fight the good fight.

Your most trusted friends on Earth are also important. You should choose them carefully. If you choose close friends who do not respect God's rules, you run the risk of siding with those deceived by the Enemy. Good, virtuous friends, however, can help you endure the battle by their example and encouragement, reminding you of God's presence when you may forget.

Pledging the Heart

When we see God as a loving Father, our trust in Him will be secure. The more we trust Him, the more we can pledge our hearts to God's law of love.

Do you own the truth in your heart? God is calling you to trust Him. He is calling you, His son or daughter, to inherit His law of love.

Points to Ponder:
1. Name 1 or 2 rules that you thought were meaningless as a child, but came to understand as significant as you grow older. Can you appreciate that those rules were for your good, even if you couldn't understand them?
2. Do you defend your Faith? Think of a way to do that this week. Can you think of anyone who bravely stands up for the truth? Find a faithful, virtuous friend who can walk with you.

Mission: Spend some time in the chapel or in a quiet space where you can speak honestly before God. Address God as Father, and in your heart, ask, "How can I own the truth? What are my questions? To whom can I go for answers in my family or in my Church?" Then ask the Holy Spirit to help you embrace your deepest identity as a beloved child of the Father. Thank Him for His work in your life, and ask Him to be with you on your journey of faith. It is an adventure!

4 Entering the Battle

Don't Be a Frog

If a frog were put into a pot of boiling water, it would immediately jump out! But if the frog were lowered into nice, warm water which was gradually heated to the boiling point, the frog would remain in the pot and die without a struggle.

Don't be like a frog! It is sometimes easy to fall prey to the lies of the Enemy. Maybe at first we make excuses for little venial sins **(warm)**. Soon, they become habits **(warmer)**. Then, we convince ourselves that we are in control **(hot)**. Moreover, we start to think that the lies of the Enemy make sense **(hotter)**. Finally, we give our full consent to the Enemy **(boiling)**, until, at last, our hearts die within us. Don't remain ignorant of the sins that have the power to stop your heart. Be sensitive to what pulls you in the wrong direction, and flee those situations.

Would soldiers enter a battlefield blindfolded? No! They would be vigilant, keeping a lookout in all directions before entering the fray. So should you. Learn the terrain. Know how the Enemy thinks. Listen for alarms. Always be aware of your spiritual environment.

> "You have made us for yourself, O Lord, and our hearts are restless until they rest in thee."
> —*St. Augustine, Confessions, Book I*

The Restless Heart

St. Augustine knew what it was like to fall prey to the lies around him. He spent his youth seeking the pleasures the world offered, ignoring the inner movements of his heart. As he grew up, he pursued popularity, luxuries, lust, and comfort, but realized that none satisfied his restless heart. His spiritual environment was deadly.

Finding himself terribly unhappy with his choices, he was sitting in a garden one day with a Bible in his hand, wrestling with the emptiness in his heart.

On the other side of the garden wall, he heard children singing a refrain: "Pick up and read." So, Augustine took up the Bible and read. His heart suddenly burned with the truth of the Gospel. He was moved to embrace Jesus Christ and His Church and to abandon his life of sin and pride.

This conversion led him to become a great theologian of the Church. He helped to convert the hearts of many, and his wisdom shaped not only the Church, but all of Western culture.

Holiness: Wholeness and Integrity

When bodily actions **match** the ethos of the heart

Marching Orders

There is a lot at stake as you enter into the battle for your heart. Your orders are finalized: you are to become a saint! Saints are like war heroes in the army of God. You might think, "I could never be a saint! I'm too young! I'm not holy enough!" But the saints themselves assure us—the smaller you are, and the weaker you feel, the greater your chances for achieving holiness! Because in Christ, "when I am weak, then I am strong" (2 Cor. 12:10). But what is holiness?

You, as a soldier in training, already know the drill: holiness is union between body and spirit. In other words, you have a well-formed conscience, you "own" the truth in your heart, and you follow that truth with your bodily actions. For instance, you know the truth that disrespecting a teacher is wrong, and what's more, you have accepted that in your heart. When tempted, your bodily actions follow the truth, and you show kindness to your teacher. That's holiness, and holiness is linked to purity of heart.

> "'Purity' of heart is gained by the one who knows *how to be consistently demanding* from his 'heart': from his 'heart' and from his 'body.'"
> *Theology of the Body 43:5*

Sin: Brokenness and Detachment

*When bodily actions **clash against** the ethos of the heart*

We Need a Medic!

Even when you have the *ethos* of the heart, you can still commit actions that contradict your well-formed conscience. This is caused by detachment, or a split between body and heart. For example, a young man might know that the Second Commandment teaches respect for the name of the Lord. Nevertheless, he tries to impress his friends by taking God's name in vain. The split between what he knows to be right and the bodily action that contradicted it, is where sin resides. This split brings disunion and sadness.

But one can always return to the fight for sainthood. The priest who offers you the Sacrament of Reconciliation is like a medic who does field surgery; he extends God's forgiveness which makes you whole again. Even when you are knocked down in battle over and over and over, you can get up and fight again. It is not easy; it is war. A faithful soldier never deserts or gives up the fight. Remember, through God's grace, St. Augustine overcame sin. You, too, can experience the victory of holiness.

Based on Gen 3:7-8 and TOB 24:3-4. © Copyright 2013 by Monica Ashour. All rights reserved.

> "The 'pure' value of man does not contain an inner break and antithesis between what is spiritual and what is sensible."
>
> *Theology of the Body 13:1*

Training for Freedom

To be a saint is to be free. The saints show us that freedom from sin allows them to become more, not less, of who they were created to be. How can we unshackle ourselves from sin to become more of who we are? The answer lies in the virtue of self-mastery. Self-mastery means knowing and doing what is right, especially in the face of temptation. Just as push-ups and weight-lifting strengthen your body, so self-mastery strengthens your heart.

What does self-mastery look like? Instead of sharing the gossip at lunch with all your friends, self-mastery allows you to change the subject. Instead of making yourself scarce when your dad is cooking dinner, you volunteer to help. Instead of procrastinating on that science fair project, you tackle it head-on.

The next time you face a temptation, listen for the still, small voice of the Holy Spirit in order to avoid splitting your bodily actions from your heart. Whether by His voice, or some other means, God is calling you to live in freedom.

Training for Love

Along with self-mastery, St. John Paul says you also should develop reverence—wonder and awe for others and yourself. Because everyBODY is created in the image of God, each person deserves reverence.

In fact, reverence points to your future vocation, which is to love. You are in training to love when you develop the habit of reverence in your attractions.

It is normal and good for men and women to be attracted to each other. But attraction without reverence can turn into lust. Lust is a form of use, the opposite of love. This is why lust is so damaging—it is based on self-gratification rather than reverence for the other. Your heart is a battlefield where reverence and use are at war with each other. Which one will win?

Reverence vs. Use

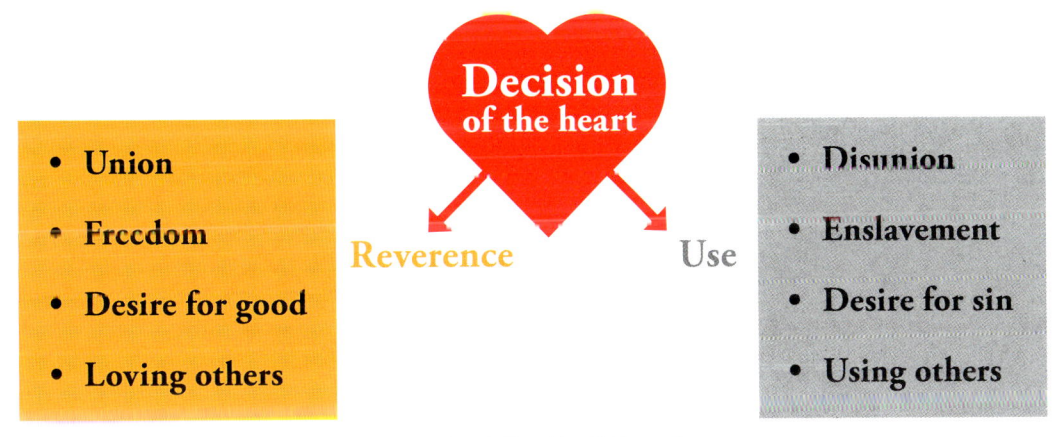

Decision of the heart

Reverence
- Union
- Freedom
- Desire for good
- Loving others

Use
- Disunion
- Enslavement
- Desire for sin
- Using others

© Copyright 2019 by Monica Ashour. All rights reserved.

The Right Path

Attraction is a good gift from God, but sometimes it can be confusing. It is easy to be carried away by thoughts of someone you admire. But the one you are attracted to deserves reverence; do not allow the sin of lust to make its home in your heart. Lust can lead to impure bodily actions, impeding real love. Work on self-mastery and reverence to stay on the right path.

Another danger is feeding an overly romantic imagination. Creating a dream-world centered around you and your "crush" is not a sign of reverence. There is nothing wrong with hoping and dreaming about a future relationship, but concupiscence can invade your hopes and turn them into a place of escape. Be careful not to fall into the common trap of creating unrealistic fantasies about another person. (Things like movies, teen novels, TV shows, and online fantasies contribute to this.) Stay grounded in reality.

> "**The reverence** born in man for everything bodily and sexual, both in himself and in every other human being, male and female, turns out to be the most essential power for keeping the body 'with holiness.'"
>
> *Theology of the Body 54:4*

The Path to Freedom

Along the path to freedom lie many dangers. Do you have a strategy for when you find yourself tempted to step off the path?

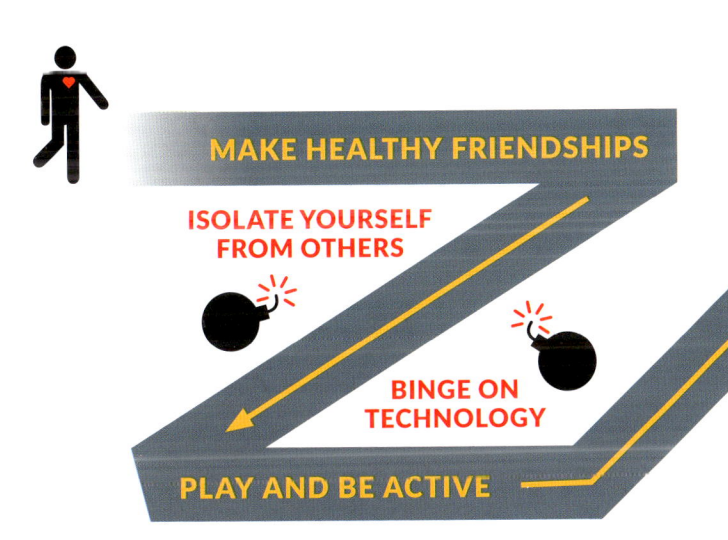

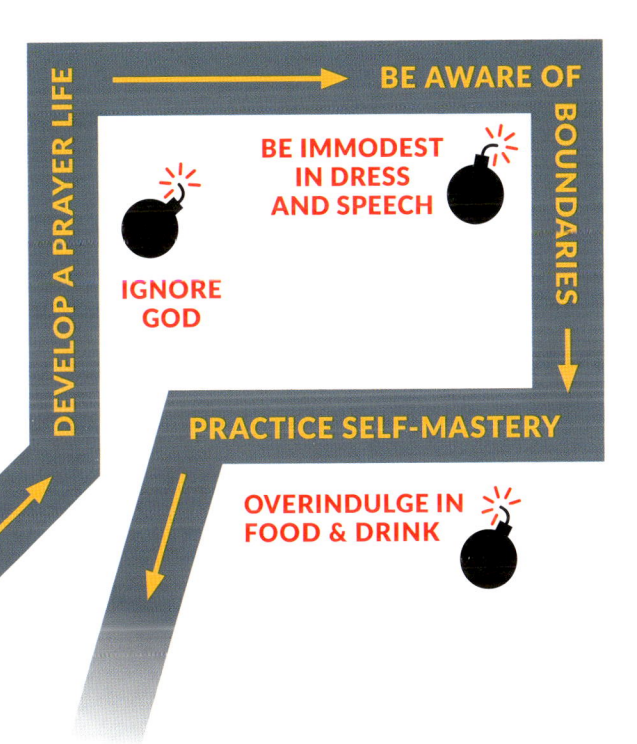

MAKE HEALTHY FRIENDSHIPS

ISOLATE YOURSELF FROM OTHERS

BINGE ON TECHNOLOGY

PLAY AND BE ACTIVE

DEVELOP A PRAYER LIFE

IGNORE GOD

BE IMMODEST IN DRESS AND SPEECH

BE AWARE OF BOUNDARIES

PRACTICE SELF-MASTERY

OVERINDULGE IN FOOD & DRINK

DANGER! EXPLOSIVES!

FREEDOM TO LOVE

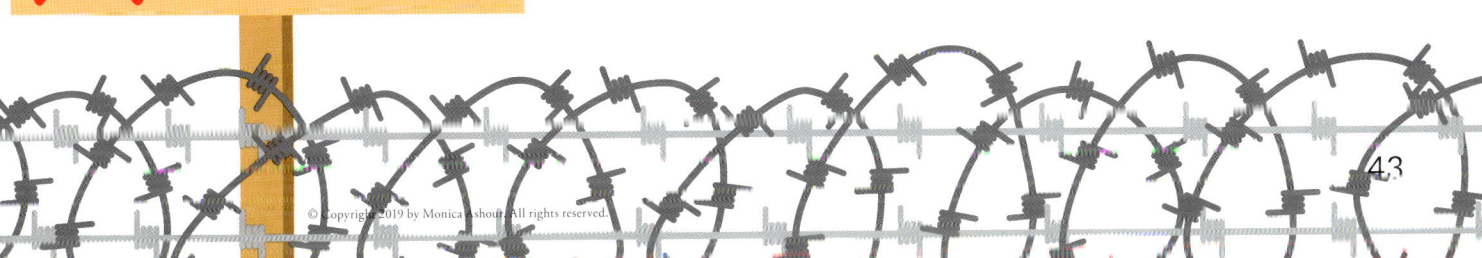

> "Blessed are the clean of heart, for they will see God."   Mt. 5:8

A Light in the Darkness

For some people, lust is a long battle, but there are strategies you can learn now to fight against this temptation. Be honest with yourself. Are there sources of temptation in your life? Perhaps a cell phone, a laptop in your room, a certain T.V. show, or even a group of people?

Do not hide in darkness, but shine a light on all areas where you are tempted. Examine all the corners of your heart. Be extremely alert in your teen years as this is the crucial time to win the battle for your heart. What can you do to rid yourself of those areas where you might be overcome by temptation?

> "Purity is a requirement of love. It is the dimension of the inner truth of love in man's 'heart.'"
> *Theology of the Body 49:7*

True Freedom

Think about the first time you learned to ride a bike without training wheels. Remember how good that felt? You found your balance as you rode faster and faster. You felt the wind on your face and heard your parents cheering proudly. That was an experience of freedom! When you practice self-mastery, you also experience freedom. The more you learn to reject sin, the more you free your heart to love.

Consider for a moment—what is your experience when you give in to sin? That anxious, guilty feeling warns you that something is wrong. St. John Paul says that sin "suffocates" freedom in the heart. But when you turn from the habit of sin, even for the very first time, you experience freedom and the truth of your identity as a son or daughter of God.

So don't stay enslaved. You are made for freedom. You are made to be a gift. You are made to experience your real self—a free self.

Healed Heart

It is not just our own sins that wound the heart. We are also hurt by the mistakes and frailties of others, from their harsh words to their betrayals. In Heaven, our hearts will be perfectly healed, for we will be perfectly known by all. But for now, you can be boldly courageous—which literally means "brave of heart"—for God accepts you completely. Jesus offers you His Sacred Heart to heal your broken heart.

45

Jesus' Sacred Heart

A lifelong habit of devotion to Jesus' Sacred Heart will help you in your fight with concupiscence. Why do we foster a devotion to His Heart? Why not to His brain or to His eyes?

It's because the Sacred Heart of Jesus is the source of mercy. His cross, His crown of thorns, and His pierced side remind you of the great sacrifice Christ willingly made for you. The fire is a symbol of purifying love burning for you. Jesus knows better than anyone how to win the battle of the heart. In fact, He has already won! You need only to enter into His victory. How? By choosing to love God and others with the Heart of Christ.

Mary's Immaculate Heart

The heart of Our Lady is united with the Heart of her Son, Jesus. Her heart suffered with Him during His agony on the Cross and then rejoiced with Him when He rose from the dead.

Mary's Immaculate Heart is depicted with roses to symbolize purity, but is pierced by a sword to symbolize her *compassion*, which means "to suffer with." Just as she suffered with her Son, Mother Mary suffers with you during your hard times. She is the ultimate model of the Christian soldier—strong, steadfast, and unwavering in doing the Father's will.

> "The purity of heart required for love is achieved in the first place through union with God in prayer. When God's grace touches us, this also produces a path to pure, undivided human love."
>
> YOUCAT 463

> "**This, then, is the essential and fundamental 'power':** *the love planted in the heart* **('poured out in our hearts')** *by the Holy Spirit*." *Theology of the Body 126:5*

Divine Mercy

St. John Paul teaches us that despite our failings and sin, we should not be discouraged. He knows the process of purification is difficult, but we can take heart. If we cooperate with the Holy Spirit, our hearts will be made pure.

In 1931, Jesus revealed Himself to St. Faustina as the image of Divine Mercy, with blood and water streaming from His Heart to the world. Christ told St. Faustina that one drop of His Blood would have been enough to save all sinners. We can be sure that Christ's Heart is for all who are sick, sore, and wounded. Do you feel too sinful for Him? Do you feel too bad, ugly, or hurt? Here's the Good News: like water, mercy flows to the lowest point! It is precisely your imperfections, not your perfections, to which God is drawn. Won't you allow His Divine Mercy into your heart?

Winning the Battle

Each time you form an alliance with the Holy Spirit in your heart, you have the power to resist temptation. The experience of true freedom in Christ will be yours. You will be freed for love. "For freedom Christ set us free" (Gal. 5:1).

So, when the battle for your heart is raging, follow these steps:
- First, examine the inner movements of your heart. *Know the battlefield!*
- Next, form your heart, guided by the Church. *Study the battleplan!*
- Then, choose to own the truth in your heart. *Accept your orders!*
- Finally, practice self-mastery and reverence. *Fight the good fight!*

Then you will have proven yourself a true solider for Christ on the battlefield of your heart, and you will share in His victory. The Purple Heart for valor will be yours for all eternity.

Points to Ponder:
1. Imagine your life as a saint. St. Luke is the patron saint of doctors, St. Monica of mothers. What would you be the patron saint of?
2. How can you begin to live in self-mastery and reverence?

Mission: Try St. Benedict's ancient prayer form, *Lectio Divina*: **1. Read.** Imagine yourself in a scene from the Bible. **2. Meditate.** What phrase from that scene strikes you? **3. Contemplate.** Sit silently in the presence of God. Have a heart-to-Heart communion with Him.